STOCK MARKET INVESTING FOR BEGINNERS: A COMPLETE GUIDE TO TRADING LIKE A PROFESSIONAL

LEARN TO INVEST IN STOCK MARKET FROM FUNDAMENTALS & VALUE INVESTING TO TECHNICAL ANALYSIS & TRADING STRATEGIES

WWW.INVESTINGPRODIGY.COM

Contents

INTRODUCTION: 1

CHAPTER 1: CONFLICTING STOCK INVESTING ADVICE THAT'S PREVENTING YOU FROM MAKING MONEY 4

    Growth Stocks Are Traded Differently Than Value Stocks 6

    Fundamental Analysis Entry Points Are Different Than Technical Analysis Entry Point 8

    Investing Concept Is Different Than Trading Concept 9

    Prevent Loss vs. Buy On Dips 10

    Summary 11

CHAPTER 2: PROFESSIONAL TRADERS KNOW THIS & SO SHOULD YOU! 16

    Professional Traders Vs. Casual Traders 16

    You Must Have A Trading System 19

    Invest In A Business But Trade A Stock 21

    Research The Proper Way-Don't Buy The Hype 22

    Price Is Baked Into The Value 23

    High Stock Price Is Not Expensive/Low Stock Price Is Not Cheap 26

CHAPTER 3: SET UP TO TRADE 28

    Best Demo/Paper Trading Sites 28

CHAPTER 4: HOW TO FIND THE RIGHT STOCKS TO INVEST IN! 35

    Guide To Finding The Right Stock In The Stock Market 35

    Narrowing Down The Best Stocks 40

    Summary: 42

CHAPTER 5: VALUING YOUR STOCK PICK-FINDING THE PRICE YOUR STOCK IS ACTUALLY WORTH 44

Value Of Your Stock vs. Current Price (Is It A Good Buy?) 46
Valuation Calculation Formula 1: 48
Valuation Calculation Formula 2 53
Summary 61
CHAPTER 6 TECHNICAL ANALYSIS -LEARN GOOD ENTRY POINT AND STOCK TRADING 63
charts 64
Indicators 66
Summary 72
CHAPTER 7: POWERFUL TESTED STRATEGIES YOU CAN TRADE ON TODAY! . 74
Strategy 1 75
Strategy 2 78
Strategy 3 79
Strategy 4 81
Strategy 5 84
Strategy 6 86
Strategy 7 88
Strategy 8 90
IN SUMMARY -UNDERSTAND THE WHOLE SYSTEM 94

INTRODUCTION:

This book is written to take a beginning investor, someone who is starting to invest in the stock market or has dabbled in the stock market without much success and introduce them to a complete trading system that many professional traders use!

This book covers all aspects of investing/trading and will cut years of wasteful learning and misleading truth. I've attempted to summarize and introduce you to most widely used trading methodology used by experience traders.

In the past, there wasn't access to good information, you had to go to library or you had to subscribe to newspaper just to read stock table in the back of business section of the newspaper. Then had to get on the telephone (not cell phone) with your broker just to buy a stock. The problem today is just the opposite. One there is abundance of information to sort through, second there is way too much conflicting, misleading and salesy information. I call this "feel good" information. It will promise you the world, make general theoretical pitches, about becoming a millionaire and retiring on the beach, all for low price of $19.99 without teaching you anything!

I'll leave it up to you to decipher the good information from the bad. Your aim should be to learn, apply and get results! Whether this information comes in form of flashy salesy new website or crumbled up piece of paper! FOCUS ON THE CONTENT!

This book lays the foundation you can build on, simplifies the process and takes the noise out. You will see things differently even after the 1st chapter.

You see, most professional traders use a trading/investing system, they don't haphazardly go in and out of trades. They trust their system and they don't buy or sell just because someone tells them to, they do their research. They see the numbers companies are producing, make sense of them and apply them to their trading system. They understand the price of the stock and value of the stocks are different. In addition to numbers, they also use technical analysis and indicators to get in and out at the right time.

In this book, you will learn how to find the right stocks, narrow them down and get the right numbers out of the company. You will learn how to calculate the true value of the company. Once you know how much the company is worth, you can calculate its stock price and decide if it will be a good or a bad buy! This book will show you where you can find this information for your favorite company/stock and walks you through step-by-step calculation to derive at its true value. This is how professional investors find great long-term investment for fraction of its true value.

On the other hand, not all stocks are great investment, some stocks move in pattern & would make great short-term trades. You can profit from these patterns by applying technical analysis such as charting, indicators and strategies. This book includes trading strategies that few books share.

All these items are covered to give you comprehensive, all-inclusive trading methodology.

Enough fluff, Let's get started...

CHAPTER 1: CONFLICTING STOCK INVESTING ADVICE THAT'S PREVENTING YOU FROM MAKING MONEY

This chapter alone will save you years of wasted learning, prevent confusion and lots of money down the drain. It took me 10 years to figure this out on my own, going around and around and going nowhere!

You know that when you sell your stock, someone is buying it from you. When you buy your stock, someone is selling it to you. This means there are investors out there that are thinking completely contrary to you. Are they misguided, or are you? Someone has to be wrong……right?

This is because there is too much information, too many methods, too many opinions out there! I didn't know where to start! I realized whatever method I just learned, there is a method that is 100% contradicting to what I just learned, so which is the right one? I would learn a method only for that method to be debunked short after. I found myself all over the place trying different things.

There were sleazy salesy/workshop selling me garbage (green arrow I buy/red arrow I sell, with no explanation as to what they meant). Then there were honest people who swear by their system, but they are in direct contradiction by other honest people who swear by their system! Finally, there were sites/blogs that have way too much data, they look impressive, but I have no idea how to make any sense of the information they provided. As a novice investor I didn't know where to start.

Imagine you have two friends who have each made billions from the stock market, both are sincere in teaching you how to invest/trade. You are learning from both, the only problem is, anytime there is a shift in the market one of them tells you to buy and the other tells you to sell! You want to trust them both, so sometimes you follow one's advice and other time you follow the others, but you aren't making any money!

I would advices you not to follow someone's advice blindly, follow a certain principal or create a trading system, <u>without understanding it!</u> You will be all over the place, and when their system fails you won't be able to modify it since you didn't learn how the system worked in the first place! This is why I'm against someone touting stock picks or have this one strategy that has made them millions. If they totally convinced you, you can try their system on the side, but focus on learning for the long term, and stock piling blocks of knowledge...you will be better off in long run! Let me attempt to cut out 10 years of noise in next 3 pages!

GROWTH STOCKS ARE TRADED DIFFERENTLY THAN VALUE STOCKS

There is a very popular saying in the stock market "Don't try to catch a falling knife". This means never buy a stock that is falling! As you can imagine the stock may continue to fall and can possibly bankrupt you! I once bought a stock that I didn't sell as it was coming down. It went all the way down and then became worthless! The commission to sell the stock cost me more than what the stock was worth! I couldn't sell the stock and it was a bitter reminder every time I logged in and saw my investment had turned into $.000012! I had to call my broker to remove security from showing up in my portfolio.

In 1999 there were many dot com companies that never made it back. When the stock market was crashing, if you continued buying into investment that was falling you may have dumped good money after bad and lost it all! NASDAQ ETF QQQ was $120 in early 2000 then it tanked for 2 years, all the way down to around $20 in 2002. It did not rise over $120 until 2016! If you held on to that ETF in 1999 and continued buying on its way down, at some point you may have run out of money. On top of that you didn't breakeven for up to 17 years! That means for 17 years you made 0% on your investment! Now could that money be invested elsewhere for better returns?

In 2008, same thing happened again to lesser effect. I'm not singling out a stock, I'm talking about general market (many stocks)! It holds true even if you stuck to your ETFs, mutual funds and indices index.

In 2000 and in 2008, some of my stock investment became worthless and I lost money. I learned I will never hold on to a stock that is falling, or just teeter tottering again! I will only invest in stocks that are rising day after day and will sell & get out if the stock is not moving up or turns down. Why would I ever invest in a security that is or has fallen so much when I can get out and wait for the market to start going up again (Growth investing)?

Then I learned that's exactly what Warren Buffet and other millionaire investors do! Warren Buffet looks at these stocks as a good bargain, he buys them when they have fallen and everyone else is selling, below what they are worth (value investing). One of his famous quotes "Price is what you pay. Value is what you get"!

At this time, you should be asking yourself:

"SO…DO I BUY WHEN THE STOCK PRICE COMES DOWN OR DO I SELL?"

There are books written arguing growth vs. value investing. I don't want to make a case which is better but want you to understand this concept. Otherwise, you will hear different guru's (Warren Buffet vs. William O'Neil) telling you different things, that will put you in conflicting buy/sell zones and you will be all over the place!

FUNDAMENTAL ANALYSIS ENTRY POINTS ARE DIFFERENT THAN TECHNICAL ANALYSIS ENTRY POINT

Fundamental analyst will tell you the best way to invest in a company is to figure out how the company is doing (by its performance) by studying its cash flow, earnings, expenses, assets and liabilities; all of which can be found in its 10k to give you better understanding of the overall status of the company. If the stock value is right, then buy and hold! Then as the company grows, so will your shares. They are not concern about short-term trending up or down.

Technical analyst focuses on the stock's chart pattern, trendlines, moving averages, support and resistance and many other indicators all of which gives you clue into when to buy and sell stocks. Technical analysts usually aren't concerned with who is running the company, what their annual report or 10k states.

These two methods could trigger different buy/sell points contradicting each other on when to enter and exit a trade. I will show you how to find great companies, run the numbers, do the fundamental analysis then apply technical analysis on them. We will learn both and then incorporate them into one system.

INVESTING CONCEPT IS DIFFERENT THAN TRADING CONCEPT

There is a difference between short-term trading and long-term investing. When you invest in a company, you are hoping to reap the profits as that company builds wealth over a longer period. You are hoping the company will be worth a lot more in the future through ups and downs. The theory is that as company grows so will its overall value and in turn your investment in it. This requires some forecasting and usually a buy and hold strategy, as it will take some time for the company to grow.

Trading involves short-term buying and selling of a security. You are hoping to take advantage of the short-term gain or a trend and get in & out of positions relatively quickly. You are hoping to beat "buy and hold" strategy which is usually implemented with longer term investing. You are less concerned of the long-term prognosis of the company.

You can see how a great short-term trading opportunity maybe triggering different buy/sell signals than long-term buy and hold strategy.

In this book I will use investing and trading interchangeably but understand that trading is usually short-term, and investing is usually long-term.

PREVENT LOSS VS. BUY ON DIPS

Should you buy on dips or place a stop loss to avoid bigger loss? These two methods can also trigger different buy/sell signals. While one analyst buys every time there is a dip, because they see the dip as a buying opportunity to buy a stock for less. Another analyst is afraid that it could be on its way down and wants to prevent further loss and gets out. If the market comes up after the dip the first analyst will have bragging right for buying at a lower price. However, if the market dip turns into bear market, the second analyst will argue that getting out early was the right decision. Who is right? I don't know a lot more goes into their call, but you can again see different buy/sell signals here.

MINDSET

Another decision to buy or sell could also depend on investor's mindset.

For example:

Let's say there are two investors. Investor 1 bought FB at $22 and see its rise to $200. FB then drops to $150, investor 1 panics that stock could go way down and figures he has made enough profit and he sells it to prevent further loss. Investor 2 is late to the game, she starts using Facebook and finds out it would be great company to own and sees the stock was at $200 and has now come down to $150, she figures it's a perfect buying opportunity at a bargain price and buys it at $150. One investor sold at $150 and the other investor bought at $150. Now FB as a company doesn't care if you bought it at $22 or at $150, it's going to do what it does. Whether you think it's a great buy or bad buy, that's your opinion! This is why it doesn't only matter what you think, it matters what the numbers says! How do you know it's a great buy?

SUMMARY

The point I'm trying to make to all my beginner investors is you will be very confused when you listen to all arguments about when you should buy and when you should sell, you will get your head spinning! You will be following these guru's blindly and completely reliant on their opinion.

Can you see all the contradictory methods of when you should buy and when you should sell? Now multiply this by millions of people who adhere to certain strategy and swear by it and are going to influence you!

As I mentioned before, when you are selling a security someone on the other side is buying and vice versa! Some wants out and others want in at that same price. They may have different investment styles and philosophies. My point is for you to recognize different buy/sell signals based on various strategies and methods being used. You will waste years and years of learning if you don't understand this principal and don't stick by it!

So here is the answer!
When you are learning to trade or invest in stocks don't trade haphazardly or buy/sell because your colleagues/friends or someone online is telling you to do it. The only way to combat this is for you to learn, create a trading plan, a philosophy that you believe in, that you monitor & back-tested it and most of all is showing you results!

Ask yourself:
Are you long-term or short-term investor?

Are you basing your decision on charting, indicators?

Are you basing your decision on reading 10k?

Are you a value investor?

A growth investor?

Are you buying on potential?

If the stock doesn't behave like you want it to, when will you get out? Or will you double down? Why? Why not?

Most importantly monitor all your trades. I use excel spreadsheet that has all my loss and profits and reason why for my entry and exit.

Bottom line, is you need to create a trading plan/system, don't trade haphazardly! You can change your system if it's not working for you but give it some time and see if it's working for you!

Chapter 2: Before we create a whole trading plan, let's discuss other differences between professional and casual traders.

LEARN MORE AT:
WWW.INVESTINGPRODIGY.COM

ⓒ Copyright 2016 - All rights reserved. -DISCLAIMER

Please read the Disclaimer carefully before you start to read the rest of the book. By reading this book you accept and agree to be bound and abide by the Disclaimer. If you do not want to agree please do not purchase the book or ask for a refund.

Do not base any investment decision upon any matter found in this book. I'm not registered as a securities broker-dealer or an investment adviser either with the U.S. Securities and Exchange Commission or with any state securities regulatory authority. I'm neither licensed nor qualified to provide investment advice.

FOR EDUCATIONAL AND INFORMATIONAL PURPOSES ONLY: This content is intended to be used for informational purposes only. It is very important to do your research and analysis before making any investment, based on your own personal circumstances. You should take independent financial advice from a professional in connection with, or independently research and verify, any information that you find in this book and wish to rely on, whether for the purpose of making an investment decision or otherwise.

Please remember that past performance may not be indicative of future results. Different types of investments involve varying degrees of risk, and there can be no assurance that the future performance of any specific investment, investment strategy, or product made reference to directly or indirectly in this book, will be profitable, equal any corresponding indicated historical performance level(s), or be suitable for your portfolio. Due to various factors, including changing market conditions, the content may no longer be reflective of current opinions or positions. Moreover, you should not assume that any discussion or information contained in this book serves as the receipt of, or as a substitute for, personalized investment advice. to the extent that a reader has any questions regarding the applicability of any specific issue discussed below to his/her individual situation, he/she is encouraged to consult with the professional advisor of his/her choosing.

NOT LEGAL ADVICE: I have done my best to ensure that the information provided in this book is accurate and provide valuable information. Regardless of anything to the contrary, nothing available on or through this book should be understood as a recommendation that you should not consult with an attorney and/or registered financial advisor to address your particular situation. I recommend that you seek advice from an attorney and/or registered financial advisor prior to taking any actions.
I shall not be held liable or responsible for any errors or omissions in this book or for any damage you may suffer as a result of failing to seek competent legal advice from a licensed attorney and/or financial advisor who is familiar with your situation.

NO PROFESSIONAL-CLIENT RELATIONSHIP: Your use of this book does not create a professional-client relationship between you and the me. Thus, you recognize and agree that we have not created any professional-client relationship by the use of this book or any resources through it.

USER'S PERSONAL RESPONSIBILITY: By using this book, you accept personal responsibility for the results of your actions. You agree to take full responsibility for any harm or damage you suffer as a result of the use, or non-use, of the information available in this book or the resources available by or through it. You agree to use judgment and conduct due diligence before taking any action or implementing any plan or policy suggested or recommended in this book.

NO GUARANTEES: You agree that I have not made any guarantees about the results of taking any action, whether recommended in this book or not. I provide educational and informational resources that are intended to help users who read this book based on my experience and opinions only. You nevertheless recognize that your ultimate success or failure will be the result of your own efforts, your particular situation, and innumerable other circumstances beyond the control and/or knowledge by me. You also recognize that prior results do not guarantee a similar outcome. Thus, the results obtained by me or other recommended in this book or otherwise – applying the principles set out in this book are no guarantee that you or any other person or entity will be able to obtain similar results.

ERRORS AND OMISSIONS: This book is intended, but not promised or guaranteed, to be correct, complete, and up-to-date. I have taken reasonable steps to ensure that the information contained in this book is accurate, but I cannot represent that this book is free of errors. You accept that the information contained in this book may be erroneous and agree to conduct due diligence to verify any information obtained from this Website and/or resources available prior to taking any action. You expressly agree not to rely upon any information contained in this book without doing your due diligence.

Reproduction: In no way is it legal to reproduce, duplicate, or transmit any part of this document in either electronic means or in printed format. Recording of this publication is strictly prohibited and any storage of this document is not allowed unless with written permission from the publisher. All rights reserved. The information provided herein is stated to be truthful and consistent, in that any liability, in terms of inattention or otherwise, by any usage or abuse of any policies, processes, or directions contained within is the solitary and utter responsibility of the recipient reader. Under no circumstances will any legal responsibility or blame be held against the publisher for any reparation, damages, or monetary loss due to the information herein, either directly or indirectly.

Respective authors own all copyrights not held by the publisher.
The information herein is offered for informational purposes solely and is universal as so. The presentation of the information is without contract or any type of guarantee assurance. The trademarks that are used are without any consent, and the publication of the trademark is without permission or backing by the trademark owner. All trademarks and brands within this book are for clarifying purposes only and are the owned by the owners themselves, not affiliated with this document.

CHAPTER 2: PROFESSIONAL TRADERS KNOW THIS & SO SHOULD YOU!

PROFESSIONAL TRADERS VS. CASUAL TRADERS

All advance traders understand this and so should you! There is no 100% guarantee that you will have all wins, unless you have inside information on stock (which is illegal)! You can do all the research in the world, but you can't 100% accurately guarantee all your trades will be profitable. It's hard to predict the market because nobody has full control of everything. There are things that are outside of everyone's control. No one entity can control news, events, disasters, fraudulent management, feds raising/lowering the rates, food borne poisoning at fast food chain restaurant, oil spill, lawsuit, announcing new CEO, airplane crash, bad earning and the list goes on and on.

The question you should ask is, if this happened to the company you have invested in, what will you do?

Are you a value investor, who is going to purchase more as the company's stock goes down, knowing company will recover? Are you investing for long-term? Are you basing it on a chart (that you have back tested)? Is it still a great company? Or are you going to sell and cut your losses?

Most casual trader may be unaware of the news, or they hear news and go to financial websites to reads couple of blogs/articles looks at PE ratio and see what the analyst says: buy/hold/sell and think about it for few mins and make a call.

They will say to themselves:
"I think last time I went to shop there it was crowded and my wife shops there and she likes it!"

No offence but the market doesn't care if your wife shops there or if it was crowded last time, you were there, or the clerk was nice to you or they refunded you when they shouldn't have! Do you know their market capitalization, do you know how many chain stores there are nationwide or even internationally? A store here or there won't make much difference, you have to see a grander picture.

Other casual traders tune in to financial networks to get more news and listen to what the guru say about a recent decline in their stock. Financial networks are great at reporting the overall condition of the market and major news. I also think they are educational, and I encourage you to watch them. However, they don't really care about your specific situation and you must understand they stay in business by creating exciting stories, selling entertainment, sensationalizing stories and market condition. This is where the ratings are, period! If you tune into them too much and try to predict every next move of the market, you will go crazy!

Professional traders spend less time on general news and more time on specific news! They may rely financial networks to get some general news but don't spend all day watching CNBC, Bloomberg, etc. to see what their take is. They go straight to the source from the company's 10k, 10q, listening to their quarterly earning calls, company news, etc. This is how they evaluate their company. By the way they spend NO TIME what a blog says (unless it's coming from company's management), or what someone thinks. They do systematic research on their company, work on a system, a philosophy and rules they adhere to that they have researched/learned extensively! This keeps them in line when the market turns on them. They are not frantically buying or selling, based on other people opinion of the market. Sometimes they go against popular belief because they have researched enough and other times, they are the popular belief. They have either back tested or have fundamental reasoning and know the in/outs of the stock they own. If the story changes, they will have an exit plan, but it's based on a research, not opinion of others.

One of my colleagues, a casual trader, stated he doesn't like trading because it's no different than gambling. I do think there are aspects to investing that maybe like gambling (pure luck), however I do think there are factors that can be controlled in investing. If you learn these factors, you can minimize your risk and increase your profit over the long-term. This is not to say I or others (that I know of) have 100%-win formula, but you can definitely put the odds in your favor!

YOU MUST HAVE A TRADING SYSTEM

I'm a big proponent of creating and working in a trading system. Even if you are a novice, I encourage you to start the documenting process. As you learn more, you can modify this or add more nuance to this. You can create a stock investing journal and record keeping of your thoughts and vital information. You can start by documenting some basic things:

1. Your objective-Why are you buying this stock? (This could be several paragraphs or very concise). Is this a long-term position or a short-term position? Are you going to hold it as it tanks? Buy more? Sell? Is this clearly outlined in your plan?

2. What is your risk tolerance, as it pertains to your overall money management (Are you getting carried away

investing more than you can afford to lose?).

3. Do you have an exit plan, which outlines when/why you will get out! Is there a price point you will get out at? If it drops 10%, 20%, 50%, 80%? When will you get back in if the stock turns on you? This is part of reversal strategy- covered later. Which will prevent you from losing everything if you sell and the market turns on you and you don't get back on!

4. Document your thoughts as the price, rises and falls, and as you apply different strategies. Even if you are not trading, enter your thinking weekly, monthly, etc.

5. In addition to just your thoughts, keep tab on your wins/loss. I like to create an excel spreadsheet, that has all my trades from ticker symbol to profits and losses I have incurred. This keeps me in check, if I'm constantly losing money and major indices are making money, then I might as well invest in the indices and not trade individual stocks myself!

As you grow as an investor, you can omit basic information and add more complicated formulas, reasoning and entry/exit points to your journal.

If you are not short-term trading (we will cover short-term trading strategies later in the book) but plan to be a long-term investor, then understand that you are INVESTING in that company!

You must look at that company with long term horizon. Just as you would not buy one business today and sell it tomorrow, you are not going to buy stock of that company today and sell it tomorrow. You should believe the company you are investing in will grow in the long term…5 yrs., 10 yrs., 15 yrs. or even 20 yrs. Of course, you must also have an exit plan if the company makes major shift (CEO change, Merger, Disaster, Competition, ETC.) For the most part though you invest with mindset that you will hold position in that company for the long-term and give the company and your investment in it, a time to grow.

When you buy a stock in that company, understand that you are now the owner of that company! You have a stake in that company. Depending on how many shares you buy in that company determines the percentage of your ownership. Most of the time individual investors are very small shareholders, nonetheless you do own part of that company and you should approach your investment with the same mindset. As I mentioned before, when professional investors own company, they want to know EVERYTHING that happens in that company. (Date of earning, upper mgmt., insider trading, earning calls, etc.) and you too need to get in the habit of doing the same thing.

So instead of thinking you are a small meaningless shareholder, look at it as you are buying the whole business, the whole company, the whole enchilada! So, you better do your due diligence prior to investing any money in it. You need to connect with that business/company. You want the business to be meaningful to you, you want to connect with people managing that business (your money is at stake), you better trust them, and you want to follow them closely.

This is an important principal, that allows you to really critique and research the business before you put your hard-earned money into that business.

RESEARCH THE PROPER WAY-DON'T BUY THE HYPE

Companies are marketed to you constantly! They are being marketed on blog, on CNBC, Facebook ads, various other sites online, etc. You may not realize they are being marketed to you, but they are! Even if they are not touting a company, they will tout an industry and then ever so slightly name few good stocks within that industry. You may have stock "guru's" come in and shout out how great a stock is or suggest why a stock may do well. Facebook ads begging you to click on "THE NEXT NETFLIX", "IT'S LIKE BUYING AMAZON IN 1999", etc.!

Blogs/newsletters that totally convincing you how great the company is. They may have the right picks, or they may have ulterior motives, but how will you know? You won't, unless you do your research! Some of these blogs are malicious…as soon as you buy, they sell! It's called "Pump and Dump", others want to sell you things and I'm sure some are legitimate, but my point is, you won't know until you learn to research.

Novice investors often get taken advantage off, by a newsletter that looks too good to pass up, community forums where group or individuals are hyping up a stock, etc. I'm not saying all of them are malicious, some maybe very legit and come from a good solid place. All I'm saying is DO YOUR RESEARCH. I will show you a proper way to research based on numbers and not hype!

PRICE IS BAKED INTO THE VALUE

One of the biggest mistake novice investors make is they will see something or come across a product or service they like so they buy a stock in it. Or, because a friend or a colleague highly recommends it, or because it has dropped a lot and it must go up now. An example of this would be; I like coffee from "Starbucks", so I'll buy their stock. All of my friends use "Facebook", so I'll buy their stock. I found my spouse from "match.com" and she is so awesome, so let me invest in their stock. President Trump tweets a lot so "Tweeter" stock must go up!

The problem with this thinking is you are 1 person, maybe 2 if your friend recommended it to you, do you know a company could have billions of outstanding shares, and millions of people who have invested in those company at different price interval? Do you know that thousands of people knew about this stock before you? Do you know thousands more have invested in these securities way before you had their product or used their services? Most of how great that stock is, is already baked into the price of that stock! Most of the time (not always) you are late to the game! Accept that stock doesn't have to do anything just because now you think it's a great stock and have invested in it!

There are exceptions, if you happen to know something that an average person doesn't know (aside from insider information- which is illegal), but this is mostly not the case. I.e., startup company that you see growing locally with very little coverage, but they are expanding, or certain industry is growing, and a particular company will grow with it, etc. Keep in mind most companies you find online; others have found before you and the price is reflected in that stock.

The price is baked into the stock, because everyone wants to be the first one to invest in it. Investors start to predict and buy on rumors. Everyone wants to get in before it's too late! This is usually way before you realize you like their product or service!
Sports analogy would be like an athlete signing a contract based on his/her potential and not performance. Lebron James and Kobe Bryant signed deals for millions coming out of high school without ever playing a single game in the NBA! It wasn't their performance in the NBA, it was their potential! Similarly, investor react to rumors and buy in advance based on what a company could become. When you find out, the stock price may already have its potential baked into the price and it doesn't care that you have now realized it's potential and have entered the market. Actually, it never really cares when you enter the market-unless you are going be buying in millions. Like scouts realize the potential in an athlete before he/she becomes great, professional investors have realized a potential value in a company before it becomes profitable.

As you get better, you will able to predict and buy stocks on potential or see its value before others, but for starter stick to the actual numbers. Just understand that if you like a company's product or their service, add it to your radar, but you will need to do more research before you buy, by analyzing its numbers.

HIGH STOCK PRICE IS NOT EXPENSIVE/LOW STOCK PRICE IS NOT CHEAP

Another common misconception I hear is:

"I'm not buying that stock because the stock price is too high, it's better to invest in stocks with cheaper stock price. I.e., Google is trading at $1,200/share and it's too much, it has higher chance of coming down."

You must understand that Google may not be worth it at $1,200/share or maybe a bargain, but don't determine it **just** based on its price.

Berkshire Hathaway-BRK'A, in 1982 was selling for $485 per share! In 1982 $485 was a lot of money for a share and one may have thought it was too expensive to buy! In 1992 it was selling at $10,000/share! In 2002 it was selling at $70,000/share! In 2012 it was selling at $120,000/share. In 2019 is selling over $300,000/share! Now was this overpriced in 1982 at $485? Even if you take the cost of inflation out, this provided great return!

To understand this concept, you must understand the correlation between stock price, outstanding shares and market capitalization. This will show you how per share price is calculated vs. the value of the company. Let's take 2 companies:

Company A: Valued at $1 million (Market cap)
This company is choosing to offer to the public 10,000 shares (shares outstanding).
Thus: 1million/10k = $100/share (this is the price the company is trading at)

Company B: Is also valued at $1 million (Market cap)
This company is choosing to offer 100,000 stocks to the public for purchase.

Thus: 1 million/100 k = $10/share.

Both companies are valued at $1 million dollar. This does not mean that company A is overpriced, and company B is a bargain. It also doesn't mean that company A has higher chance of coming down and company B has higher chance of going up.

Next Chapter 3: If you have never invested or traded before, this chapter explains how to get started from scratch! If you have a brokerage account and have traded before you can skip this chapter!

CHAPTER 3: SET UP TO TRADE

BEST DEMO/PAPER TRADING SITES

If you are brand new to investing, this chapter is for you. If you have never traded a security, you may want to start by paper trading. This will mimic live trading, but it will be with fake money! It's like a trial run before the race.

You can create this account on many sites. You will be simulating live trading, with no real money. You can see how well you do. This also allows you to trade based on different strategies without having to risk anything. The simulated website will keep track of all your earnings, profit and losses as if you invested real money. You can create different portfolio and try different strategies (discussed in later chapter) and see which you feel comfortable with and are profitable.

Paper trading will ease you into real trading, you can build your confidence on how trading works, build your style and implement your strategies; because there is also no risk and allows you to practice and be bold in your trades. I would recommend you practice for six months on various sites prior to investing real money.

Here are best sites you can paper trade with at time of printing this book:

1. Avatrade
2. Tradingsim
3. Stockfuse
4. Investfly

You can also opt to do paper trading with broker sites (sites where you can do actual trading). The advantage to these sites is if you like the layout and the look and feel of it, you can then invest real money and begin real trading without learning the look and feel of a new broker.

Best broker sites that offer paper trading are:

1. Think or Swim
2. Tradestation
3. InvestorJunkie
4. Ninjatrader

Best Brokerage Accounts-What To Look For

Before you can start investing and trading your money, you will need to open a brokerage account. Once you place a trade order the broker will execute that trade for you. There are many sites that will be competing for your business, so do your research. Some of the factors to consider are the following:

- Are there any promotional deals that are being offered?

- What is the minimum investment-$500? 2,500?

- Does it provide premier tools (not only the research tools you find on free sites)?

- What other features do the brokers provide? Brokers are constantly updating features to the latest technology. For example, some provide alerts on SMS and other only provide alerts on email.

- What are the commission fees? (Typically range from $5-$10 per trade). Commission fees do add up but focus on what you are getting in return. Among many features, some less reputable brokers have higher slippage. For example, when you put a market order (order at current price), some broker will buy a security at $47.20 others may buy at $47.24, this $.04 difference (slippage) times the number of shares you are purchasing could wash away $5 you are saving on commission.

- Some brokerage accounts are geared towards advance traders, that provide little hand holding, little support but their price is reasonable and vice versa.

- APP functionality (download their app and play with it).

Below are few notable brokers who had earned the highest marks at the time of the book writing. However new ones make the list all the time so do you own research as well.

Merrill Lynch
Ally
E-trade
Ameritrade
Trade station
Interactive brokers
Charles Schwab
Fidelity

Funding your Brokerage Account

Once you have picked a brokerage, you can go their website and click on "open a new account" or "sign up" link. This will walk you through applying for new account application, where they will ask you for your social security #, driver license, employment status, etc. Make sure you are using a secure server here as you will be entering all your private information. At the end of your application, you will create your username/password. Mostly all the brokerage firms' websites should walk you through this process very easily. Once this is done you will have to fund that account by linking your checking account bank to your brokerage bank and transferring money electronically or writing a check to them. Since each firm maybe slightly different, it's best to contact the brokerage firm if you have any questions with this process. It will take few days before you see the money appear in your brokerage account, so allow some time for this.

<u>If You Never Traded, Here Are the Basics on Placing A Trade</u>

If you have had a demo account, you should be somewhat familiar with trading and the sites functionality.

Once you fund the account:

You will see several tabs, most common are below:

Account --> Summary, Balance, Account holdings/position, Activity, etc.
Trade--> Stocks/options, order status, etc.
Research --> Charts, Screener, Ratings, etc.

Once you play with these options, they should be self-explanatory.

Four most common trade orders you will be placing:

Market Order: An order to buy or sell a security at once at current market price. This type of order guarantees that the order will be executed but does not guarantee the execution price. A market order generally will execute between the current bid (for a sell order) or ask (for a buy order) price. This maybe different than last traded price you see, however, it should be close to that. If you like the stock at current price and want to own it without penny pinching this is the order you want to place.

Limit Order: An order to buy or sell a security at a specific price. If you submit a limit order to buy a stock for $50, this trade will get activated and then becomes a market order and gets executed. Since market is moving very rapidly, even though your order at $50 is activated, it may not get executed exactly at $50. Some orders may be bought for a little less or for more than $50 (i.e., $50.02 or $49.94, etc.). This is ideal trade when you are not in front of your computer or when you only want to buy/sell at a particular price point. You can place limit order and forget about it, if the order gets executed your broker will most likely email you.

<u>Stop Loss Order:</u> This type of order is usually placed to avoid further loss. It's the price you want to get out at. For example, currently you own a stock at $113, however you want to get out if the price starts to fall below $100. You would place the order to sell at $100, when the stock reaches $100 the stock becomes market order and is executed (the actual price you sell maybe few cents above/below due to market fluctuation). As the name implies, you are stopping further loss.

<u>Stop Buy Order:</u> An order that is placed at a stop price above the current market price. This order is placed generally when the stock is fluctuating at a certain price level but has not had a breakthrough. However, once you know there is a breakthrough, you anticipate the stock going much higher. For example, if the stock is fluctuating between $40-$50, however if there is a breakthrough you anticipate an uptrend to go on for a while. Therefore, you will put a stop buy at $52, if the stock starts to cross at $52, your order will get executed.

Chapter 4: Once you have your account set up and you are ready to go, we can start to find stocks to invest in. There are over 4,000 publicly traded companies, how do you find out which ones to invest in?

CHAPTER 4: HOW TO FIND THE RIGHT STOCKS TO INVEST IN!

Now the all-important question, what should you invest in?

There are approximately 4,000 companies that are actively trades in NYSE/NASDAQ. The key is to find the right stock at the right time for the right price. You only need few!

GUIDE TO FINDING THE RIGHT STOCK IN THE STOCK MARKET

<u>Word of mouth:</u>
You may be able to find a good company from a friend or a colleague's recommendation, websites/blogs, news you read, TV or something you came across and thought it would be a good buy. This may seem a little contradictory from the last chapter, but it's not! It's ok to consider these companies as a viable option, you may find gems here, just know you are not buying but considering these stocks! You will simply put it on your radar! You will never buy a stock because of someone's suggestion without doing your own research! SOMEONE'S RECOMMENDATION IS WHERE YOUR RESEARCH STARTS NOT ENDS!

The reason most of us don't do deep research is because:

1. We don't know how and what to look for!
2. It takes time and effort!

When you start deep research based on numbers/fundamentals, you will find most sites will charge you for these data. Why? Because these data matters! They are not touting stocks and selling you advertisement, they are providing you vital information! It's up to you to make sense of it! And I'm going to teach you how to make sense of it and use that data to make sound investment!

First let's find these stocks:

Look around you:
There are so many companies that are making news every day, you can find them in general news (newspaper, TV, etc.) or see local ads or look around you and see what stores are popping up. Is there a product you love, a service you can't live without? You can start to see things around you and find a company behind it. Again, we are not buying we are finding companies to do research on!

Screener:

If you still don't have a favorite, start by running a screener. Stock screeners will help you narrow your search based on criteria you are looking for. Best screeners are not the one with all the bells and whistles but the ones that give you the information you are looking for. Start by looking at a brokerage firm you signed up with, check under the "research" tab. I found the following sites have a pretty good screener if you have not yet signed up with a brokerage firm.

https://finviz.com/screener.ashx
https://www.zacks.com/screening/stock-screener
https://finance.yahoo.com/screener/

Here are default numbers that you can start with on your screener to highlight some good companies and weed out bad performers. You can modify these screener as you start to understand what each criterion means.

- Market cap greater than 100M
- P/E 5-15
- Price to book .5-1.5
- Total debt/equity for the last quarter-0-1
- Current ratio > 1.5
- Return on Equity (5yrs average) > 5
- Return on Equity (last quarter) > 5
- Growth Rate > 10%

You can broaden your search if you are not getting enough results and be more restrictive if you are getting too many results. Ultimately know, this is just a pool of stocks to start further research. It is a starting point. You are not going to just buy stocks because they appear on this list.

Investing Blogs & Websites:
You can also find some great stock picks from investing blogs and websites. However, be aware of some tempting links begging you to click on them. There are thousands of investment links on websites, blogs, apps, etc., that you can't help clicking on! It's so tempting to read a blog and buy the stock, especially when it's going to tell you the next Microsoft, Netflix, Amazon and Google! It shows you a chart if you had invested $1,000 10yrs ago, it would be worth $985,000 today! You start thinking even if they are right fractionally, you'll be fine with it! They are touting the next bitcoin, the next marijuana stock, etc. This is fast, easy and so convincing! You can always consider them, but you should also realize some of these sites are selling you a product, and the fact that you clicked on a link has already benefited them! Their picks may be right or wrong, I don't know, and you won't know either, until you breakdown that company or form a particular trading strategy (discussed later), and base your decision on your trading plan. Majority of these links are

just advertisement that are bringing in the traffic to websites. Once you read that article and there will be other hidden links. You are being sold, like a second-hand tool!

However, not all sources are bad. There are articles that may be legitimate, and raises your awareness about a company, product or the market. This maybe additional place you pick up a stock pick, you can add these to your radar for further research!

www.Investors.com

Founded by William O'Neil, the website focuses primarily on growth stock. Investor Business Daily (IBD), is a good resource to see pool of many securities that are outperforming the market. This is not a value investing method. There are many different categories/sectors/industries and use of fundamental analysis and technical analysis that may help you narrow your search.

Following sites gives you good access to lots of relevant information that can help you on your research as well.

www.Nasdaq.com

www.macrotrends.net

www.stockrow.com

www.morningstar.com (Use free version, once you get better with valuation you can move to their paid version)

Once I have narrowed down to few companies, I like to weed them out further by looking at the following criteria:

Personal responsibility?

This may sound a little too virtuous, but I personally don't like to invest in companies that don't align with what I want in this world! When I was new to investing, I once owned a tobacco stock that was making me real good money. It was hard for me to sell that stock, but ultimately, I did. I just didn't want to contribute to something I fundamentally disagreed with. What you agree or disagree is up to you, but remember when you buy a stock, you are investing your money into that business/industry/sector and hoping they grow and in turn you will share in their profit. You are contributing to their growth. If you don't want more of what that company represents in the world, why invest in them? When you are making good money, it's hard to be morally grounded, but when you have over 4,000 other companies, you can afford to be picky. In all honestly, my shares in that company is like a drop in the ocean, it didn't have any impact on them! This is just my fundamental belief. As Mohandas Gandhi said, "Be the change that you wish to see in the world." Great now that our conscious is clear, let's move on.

Investing in Long Term Prospect

When you have a list of stocks either from a screener, recommendation from other people, blogs and other trustful sources. Make sure you are clear on your trading plan. I.e., Is this a trading opportunity or a long-term investment? We will discuss trading strategies later, and you may not necessarily look for these criteria for trading opportunity.

Let's assume this is a long-term investment. In that case, you want to make sure the company is large enough, meaning it can't go under that quickly! You can get this information by simply looking at its market cap. I like to see that company that is at least 100 million or greater. Is this company reputable? Will they be going strong in 20 years? Are their products/service in demand; will they be in demand in long term? Who are their competitors and how are they doing? Do you see another company taking them over? Are they iconic? Ask all the questions that prove to you that the company has been around, will be around, faces little competition to be taken over (all companies have competition, you need to see if the threat of competition would dwarf your pick). Are they leader in their industry, how long do you see them in this role?

Upper Management/Insider Trading:
Once you weed these companies out, find out who is at the helm? Where is the captain? Is there a leader with passion or just an upper-level employee collecting a big fat paycheck? Who

is the CEO, what does he/she believe in? Is this just a job or do they really want to grow the company? First and foremost, do you find them to be honest and ethical? If they are not honest with you, then it really doesn't matter how smart they or how hard working they are! Then you want to know if they are up for the job, how are they investing your money in the company? All this matter when you want to invest in a company. The problem here is reading through the fine line. No CEO comes out and says they want to tank their company. This is where you may want to see "insider trading", does upper management own shares in that company? Are they buying/selling those shares? What price did they buy? What price did they sell? Why are they selling? Insider trading can be found at many sites like: www.nasdaq.com & www.gurufocus.com

SUMMARY:

You have just learned to screen out stocks, and do a little research on companies that you may be interested in. Once you get through this stage, you should now have handful of companies that may interest you. You have learned to use some of the resources/website that may cut your time down, weed out unwanted stocks and give you a place to start. We will now do deep research on handful of companies we think are great picks! Again, we are still not just investing in those companies yet!

Chapter 5: This will be where rubber meets the road! Get ready to dive into deep research!

LEARN IN VIDEO FORMAT AT:

WWW.INVESTINGPRODIGY.COM

CHAPTER 5: VALUING YOUR STOCK PICK-FINDING THE PRICE YOUR STOCK IS ACTUALLY WORTH

You have picked few companies that you think might be a good investment, but you aren't sure! If you were to think like a professional investor, you would probably want to know how much a company is worth before you bought it! Once you know how much a company is worth, you can then determine if it's a good or a bad buy. If you went to dealership to shop for a car, it would be nice to know what the mark-up is before you started to negotiate. SEC (Security Exchange Commission) requires a company makes their financial data available to publicly traded companies! They are showing you the numbers, it's your job to make sense of them! Now, even though so much goes into what the value of a stock (potential of a company-as discussed earlier), we will attempt to find the raw value of a company based on what they have reported!

Once I'm done with screening for few good companies. I like to see the profile of that stock (www.finance.yahoo.com), type in the stock symbol and click on profile. Read what the company does. Other sites like www.morningstar.com are very effective once you need to dive into deep data-paid subscription (which provides you 10 yrs. of data as opposed to 5 yrs.) as well. You can use their free version until you feel comfortable.

When I'm investing (not trading) in a company and I have read their profiles, I want to connect with that company! I want to know that company inside-out, I want to believe in their upper management, I want to share their passion, understand that company and maybe that industry. Once I do this, then I can better start to understand their financials, understand how to value that company, and to understand if it makes sense to invest in that company. This is all part of fundamental analysis, that will help you evaluate and see if the company is worth investing in.

Once I've done the above research, I can then get up to date information about the company by reading their newly published quarterly/annual reports. This is where I get up to date information about the company's numbers. The idea of "I think that company is great because of ... [add your own theoretical reasons]" ends here. This is also how some professional fund managers research prior to investing in a company!

What we will do next is to find out EXACTLY how much a stock is worth, using real numbers from 10k.

Just a note, if you are trading (short-term) and not investing (long-term) this may not be as important, you may get by with technical analysis and strategies (discussed later).

VALUE OF YOUR STOCK VS. CURRENT PRICE (IS IT A GOOD BUY?)

Value investors believe that a stock is worth a certain price and they go through method of valuing that stock. Valuing a stock is to find out how much that stock is worth. Not in theory but in numbers! If you are able to know how much a stock is actually worth and you know how much a stock is trading at; you can easily see if it's undervalued (stock is trading below the market price-in that case it may be a good buy) or overvalued (stock is trading higher than market price-it's overpriced and not a good buy).

Keep in mind, there are many different valuation formulas, techniques, and methods, but ultimately this is where the rubber meets the road! Frustrating part in running various valuation formulas is that they can show great disparity. It's still important that you run various valuation and then use other means to forecast its true value. This way you get a base point and a good range.

If this sounds foreign to you, don't worry I will walk you through the entire valuation, step by step.

The information and data to value a company can be found on many sites, start with your broker's site. These sites derive their values from annual & quarterly reports that are reported by the companies. If the sites don't provide the data you need, you can usually find these reports (10k or 10Q) on company you are investing website --> investor relations --> see the filings (usually at the bottom of the page).

In nutshell, you would want to find if the company is making profit after all expenses are paid. If you can keep good profits year after year, the company is growing, a profitable company is going to be able to take that money and reinvest in itself so it can grow or pay the shareholder in form of dividend.

This is where you need clear mind, get your thinking cap on! THIS IS THE TIME YOU NEED BE MOST ALERT, AND MAYBE SIT WITH PAPER AND PENCIL-Here we go, let's start with our first valuation.

VALUATION CALCULATION FORMULA 1:

This valuation method was first introduced by Buffet in 1986 Berkshire letter. The overarching principal is to find out how much free cash flow did the business earn. If we know the amount of "extra cash", positive cash flow (cash in our pocket after all other bills are paid), we can use that money to grow. This is the principal behind owner's earnings. Buffet calculated the owner's earning by opening financials on the company. This is how owner's earnings are calculated.

Owner's earning =
Reported Earning (net income from cash flow statement) + Depreciation (depreciation, depletion and amortization in cash flow statement) +/- Noncash charges (receivable/payable or employee stock compensation) - Maint. Capex (cash flow statement)

In this example, I'm using "FB" data derived from www.marketwatch.com. We will be using 12/31/2017 data.

STEP 1:

Go to www.marketwatch.com and on right side, type in ticker symbol: FB.

We will be first finding the market cap or market capitalization. This refers to the total dollar market value of a company.

On this site you can see this under overview tab (this information is available on many other sites, including your broker's site → under research tab). We will be noting the following:

1. Market Cap-550.27B
2. Shares Outstanding -2.965B (all shares owned by shareholders, that's "B" for billions, you see why your and my 100 shares doesn't move the stock price)

Note: Number you see here is the current market cap, which is probably different from what the market cap was on 12/31/2017.

Now just to make sure your math is right. You can divide the Market cap by shares outstanding, should = Price of the stock. (This may be a little off since some sites round this number off, since value may be in millions or even billions).

So, in our above example, we can take 550.27b/2.965b=$185.59 should be roughly the price of the stock at this time and it is!

STEP 2:

Next, we will click on financials and go to --> Cash flow statement and note the following:

1. Net income = 15.93B
2. Depreciation, Depletion & Amortization (they are basically a write off over the years) = 3.03B
3. Deferred Income Tax = (-377M or -.377B)
4. Account payable (money that the business owes but have not yet paid) = (138M or .138B)
5. Account Receivable = (money the business needs to collect but have not received) (1.61B)
6. Capital Expenditure - Under investing activities (money spent on acquisition for upgrade and maintenance of assets) = (-6.73B)

Now we are going to add all the above numbers

15.93B
3.03B
-.377B
.138B
-6.73B

Total =11.99B this is the owner's earning

STEP 3:

Next let's see what kind of return we feel FB can potentially have. For that we will usually look at last 10 years return and average them out to give us some sort of starting point. FB has only been around 5yrs as of 2017. FB has had return of 33.92% for the last 5yrs/annually. Do we expect this company to continue to continue to produce 33.92% annually year after year? I don't, but for lots of technology company it's not unusual. Now you can calculate this based on different percentage. You shouldn't really go less than 10% (this is the minimum you should expect in the stock market). If you are not able to make at least 10%, then it may not be worth the risk you are taking. Let's do some calculations based on different percentages:

if we are going to base it on minimum amount, we are willing to expect (10%):

Owner's earning 11.99b x 10 = 119.9b and divide it by shares outstanding (2.965b) =

119.9/2.965b=$40.44.

At 33.92%:

11.99b x 33.92 = 33.92 406.70b/2.965b = **$137.17 is the value of the stock according to our valuation 1.**

Currently (as of 12/31/17), FB price is at $186.15, will it ever come to $137.17, I don't know.

According our first valuation scenario FB is over-priced at $185.15 as of 12/31/17! Now FB may never come down to $137.17, let alone $40.44. There are lots of reason for this. As I mentioned a lot of money is poured into hope and potential. Investors are buying on potential worth of the company in the future. People are willing to pay more now for potential! Potential is sometimes caked into the price.

In this case FB is overpriced ($185) based on value investing calculation ($137). I can put FB on my alert list and once FB moves under $137.17, I will be alerted. If FB is on downward trend at that time, I won't jump in and buy but rely on my technical analysis to find a good entry point (discussed in next chapter). Until I see the turnaround/reversal I won't jump in since I really don't know how drastic the fall may be! We will cover when to get in, in next section.

VALUATION CALCULATION FORMULA 2

Discounted Cash Flow Method

Valuation 2 is based on Discounted Cash Flow. If you know the rate the company is growing, you can expect the stock price to grow in similar fashion. Growth can be measured in many ways. For example, we can look at company's revenue, dividends, GDP, sales, cash flow, price to earnings ratio, and equity. Since you are measuring the rate, the company is growing you will need series of data. This can be every quarter or every year. You can get data for any of the above growth rate and compare/contrast them to give you a better gauge.

We will revisit www.marketwatch.com to obtain this data and calculate the growth rate for "Free Cash Flow". As I mentioned earlier, if you have free cash to grow your business, it triumphs other numbers. Cash is king! You can do many things with cash, which you can't do with tied up assets.

STEP 1

Let's go back to marketwatch.com.

Ticker is FB --> Go to financial statements --> Cash Flow statement --> Click on "View Ratios" --> At the bottom of the sheet you will see "Free Cash Flow":

These are the data for FB:

2013 - 2.86B

2014 - 3.63B   26.78%

2015 - 6.08B   67.57%

2016 - 11.62B 91.19%

2017 - 17.48B 50.49%

These figures are provided for you, and may vary little bit, since the number above are rounded to two digits and on excel calculation, they are rounded to 9 digits (based on it being in billions). If you get raw data and wanted to calculate your own growth rate. Use the following formula:

(2014 Free cash flow - 2013 Free Cash Flow)/2013 Free Cash Flow

(3.63B - 2.86B) / 2.86B = 26.92% (Growth rate from 2013 to 2014).

STEP 2

Now, let's identify some terms, so you know what we are calculating here.

Year: We are going to use data for last 5 years, if you can get 10years they may give you better indication. You most likely will have to pay for this data. Check with your broker If they are providing this information to you.

Cash Flow: This is how much cash is left over for the company to reinvest in itself, we have series of data to give us a rate.

WACC Formula: Weighted Average Cost of Capital, this is minimum return I expect to earn from this company. Your calculation of how much a stock is worth in the future, depends on how much return you are expecting from this stock. As a default I like to use between 7-15% minimum return. This obviously depends on the risk for that stock. For example, if the stock is risky, I would like to earn higher return, since I'm putting higher risk on the table. FB is also a technology stock, they rise fast, and they fall faster. FB has earned great returns as of 2017. Those returns are usually not sustainable. When the company does fall, it will also fall hard, as most growth/tech companies do. Now let's say through the fall and rise, I still expect 8%-10% return here.

Discount Rate: How do you find the present value of investment that may be worth $1,000 a year from now, 2 years from now or 10 years from now? You will have to work backwards. In other words, you will have to discount this amount by a particular interest rate (WACC). Assuming WACC is at 8%, we will be discounting this by 8%.

Discount Rate Formula: $(1 + WACC)^{\text{Number of years discounted}}$ $(1 + .08)^1 = 1.08$, $(1 + .08)^2 = 1.17$, $(1 + .08)^3 = 1.26$, etc.

Present Value: Now that we know the rate and we know the future cash flow stream that we have forecasted, we can work backwards and figure out the what the current value or discount value should be. This would make sense since $1,000 now is worth more than $1,000 in 5 years, as long as WACC is greater than 0.

Present Value of Future Cash Flow: Future Value/ $(1 + WACC)^{\text{Number of years discounted}}$

Cash Flow of 2.86B at 8% a year out would be worth 2.65B.
Cash Flow of 3.63B at 8% 2 years out would be worth 3.11B.
Cash Flow of 17.48B at 8% 5 years out would be worth 11.90B.

Perpetual Growth Rate: Rate at which company will continue to grow after the foreseen horizon that we have calculated for. The perpetuity growth rate is typically between the historical inflation rate of 2-3% and the historical GDP growth rate of 4-5%. The number to use here would be 2-5%, based on what your assumption on how well this company will continue to grow. Facebook is growth stock; it hasn't reached a point where its growth has been capped. It may be more than 5 years before the stock reaches its full potential. Therefore, I'm going to use 5% here. This also depends on your horizon. How long are you planning on keeping this security? If you are going to get out before this security reaches its full potential, you can potentially raise the 5% as company is still growing.

Terminal Value: In this case, we are doing calculation on 5 series of data, however what would be the value on 10 series of data, 100 series of data or even infinite amount? Are we expecting FB to continue to grow at 8% forever? Probably not, at some point in time the company will grow as much as its going to grow, and from that point it will grow at a stable rate, using perpetual growth we will figure out its terminal value. Terminal value is sum of all cash flows from an investment after forecasted period at perpetual growth rate.

FB	2013	2014	2015	2016	2017
Year	1	2	3	4	5
Cash Flow	2.86	3.63	6.08	11.62	17.48
WACC	8%	8%	8%	8%	8%
Discount Rate	1.08	1.17	1.26	1.36	1.47
Present Value of Future Cash Flow	2.65	3.11	4.83	8.54	11.90
Perpetual Growth Rate	5%				
Terminal Value	611.80				
Sum of Present Value of Future Cash Flow	31.02				
Present Value of Terminal Cash Flow (Perpetuity)	416.38				

STEP 3

Calculation:

Terminal Value Formula: Final year of cash flow * (1 + perpetual growth rate)/ (WACC-perpetual growth rate).
=17.48b * (1 + .05)/ (.08-.05) =611.80b

Sum of Present Value of Future Cash Flow: Add up all the present value of future cash flow.
=2.65b + 3.11b + 4.83 + 8.54b + 11.90b= 31.02b

Present Value of Terminal Cash Flow: What would be the value of future cash flow at the last discount rate be worth today?

Formula: Terminal Value of cash flow/Discount rate for 2017
=611.80b/1.47b=416.38b

Total Present Value of Cash Flows: By adding the last 5 years of present value of cash flow (31.02b) + adding present value of terminal cash flow (416.38b), we have reached our total present value of cash flows.
=31.02b + 416.38b = 447.41b

Debt: This is your long-term borrowing minus cash you have on hand. Now we will deduct any debt FB has. As of printing this book (12/31/17), FB doesn't have any debt. If it, did you would deduct this from $447.41b.

Our total value of Equity is 447.41b!

But we want to know price per share. To get this number we are simply going to divide the total value of equity by outstanding shares.

=447.41b/2.96b =**$151.15 per share is value of our stock according to valuation 2.**

NOTE: THIS BOOK WAS PUBLISHED IN EARLY 2019, 2018 NUMBERS HAVE NOT COME OUT.

There are, two variables you must play with here, WACC and perpetual growth rate! As I mentioned earlier, the perpetual growth rate is usually 3-5%. If perpetual growth rate is at 4% your price comes out to be $114.98.

The higher the return you expect (WACC), the lower you need to buy the security at. For example, at 9%, the value per share would be $110.87.

Margin of Safety

Fund managers who use 100% fundamental analysis want a deeper discount than just the value they calculated. They do this by using margin of safety principal. In investing world, margin of safety is the difference between intrinsic value and its market price (not to be confused with accounting where margin of safety is the difference between sales level and break-even point). Even if FB does come down to our calculated value, most value investors want a bargain, which is they want the price to be way cheaper than the value they calculated. This is the whole premises of getting a bargain and finding value in their investment. For example, if FB calculated value is $150 roughly and you are seeking 25% discount, you may want to buy FB around $113, at 50%, you would buy it around $75. Margin of safety is like a safety net, I may not completely understand everything about the business, and it gives me a cushion by buying the security at a bargain price. This is a widely used principal amongst value investors.

SUMMARY

You can play with these two valuations to get your stock in the ball park of what you might want to pay for it. As you do more valuation you will start to see which securities are clearly a bargain and which are not!

You can add securities that have passed all other parameters but are not at your bargain price to your watch list and set alert on them through your broker. You will be alerted when the stock comes down to your bargain price and then find the right entry point to buy them.

As I mentioned before, if securities are already at a bargain price, I still don't just buy that security, but I conduct technical analysis to find the right time to buy them! I don't use valuation as a hard and fast number, but it does give me a range. In this example we valued FB range somewhere between $130 - $150 roughly. Currently as end of 2017 the price of FB is roughly $180/share. This would indicate the stock is overpriced per our valuation and would just put the stock on radar to alert us if and when it comes down below $150. Neither I or anyone can predict many things about FB or any other stocks, i.e., Scandal, lawsuits, takeover, etc. This will have a negative effect on stock. On other hand future prospect on what FB could become, takeover of smaller companies and continue growing users will have positive effect on the stock. Will it be the sole social media giant that will monopolize its industry? Hype will play into the price even if the data/earnings/sales do not. My point here is simple, valuation gives you a good clue but don't buy/sell on it alone.

Another note about valuation, is that no matter what it indicates if historically the stock price keeps teeter tottering and not going anywhere, I don't buy! In conjunction with valuation, I rely on technical analysis & charting. Once I target a company I like, I want to know when is the right time to get in and the right time to get out!

Chapter 6: I'll show you how basic charting entry/exit point can help you weed out the noise.

CHAPTER 6 TECHNICAL ANALYSIS -LEARN GOOD ENTRY POINT AND STOCK TRADING

It's easier and faster to evaluate and see the security snapshot on a chart than to read their annual report. That's not to say charting is more important, it just gives me a faster snapshot of how securities are behaving. i.e., some charts move in a pattern, which makes them more predictable, and this is seen very quickly in a chart than a financial document. Growth company that is making new high, year after year can be reflected in a chart quickly, than digging through 10 years of financial documents.

I also may not want to invest in a company for a long term, I may just want to trade a stock. Understanding technical analysis is key for traders, who are looking for short-term in/out in hopes of make a profit.

Even after you find a company you love, find the right valuation, you still just don't buy it! You now need to have a good entry point. I've seen companies that have great numbers, continue to tank (I have no idea why), maybe public doesn't know about them, maybe rumors, maybe they are hidden gems, maybe I don't have my numbers right and maybe I'm missing something,

I really don't know why. What this tells me is I can't just a buy the right company at the wrong time and wait forever for them to turnaround. Once I've done the fundamental analysis and found a company to be great, then I need to get in at the right time! This is where I use the technical analysis (charting & indicators), along with several strategies.

Technical analysis can involve many complex techniques with 100's of different indicators. I want to cut to the chase and introduce you to most widely use indicators and strategies that are most commonly used by professional investors and traders.

CHARTS

Line Chart
Line chart are simply connected with close of the day. Line charts are important when you want to take the noise out of the chart, they usually get the close of one day and the close of the next day and connect them through dotted line.

Bar Chart
These charts plot open, high, low and closing price.

Candlestick Chart
They are my favorite, since they provide the most information.

Up candle is clear or blue and down candle is red or black. Up candle means that the chart is on bull or upward trend, meaning it closed higher than it opened. Down cancel means that the chart is on bear or downward trend, meaning it closed lower than it opened. The lines extending up and the lines extending down are the high and low of the day.

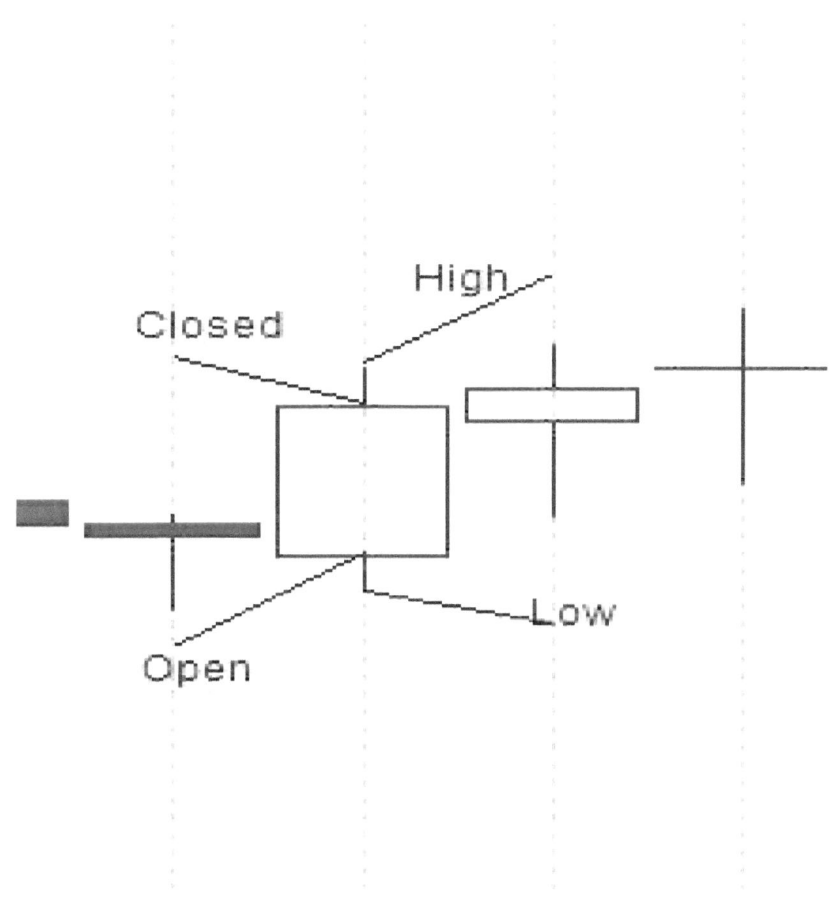

INDICATORS

MOVING AVERAGES (MAVG):

Moving averages are very popular and many, many investors and fund managers pay attention to them. Moving averages takes the price over "X" period and averages them out. This could be over 10, 20, 50, 100, 200 days. These averages help you identify the trend of stocks. In an upward trend moving averages follow the stock (are under the stock price). In downward trend these moving averages are above the stock. Thus, crossing of price and MAVG are crucial trigger point, especially to most technical traders. There are two main types of moving averages. Exponential, which will have current periods weighted more heavily and simple where all price points have equal weight. Main point to keep in mind here is if the moving average is below the stock price the stock is bullish and if the moving average is above the stock price than the stock is bearish.

In this ARLP chart you will see that when moving average is mostly under the stock the stock is on upward trend, when the moving average makes its way above the stock the stock is falling or on downward trend. Thus, the crucial point is when the moving average is crossing the stock price. This is when buying and selling happens.

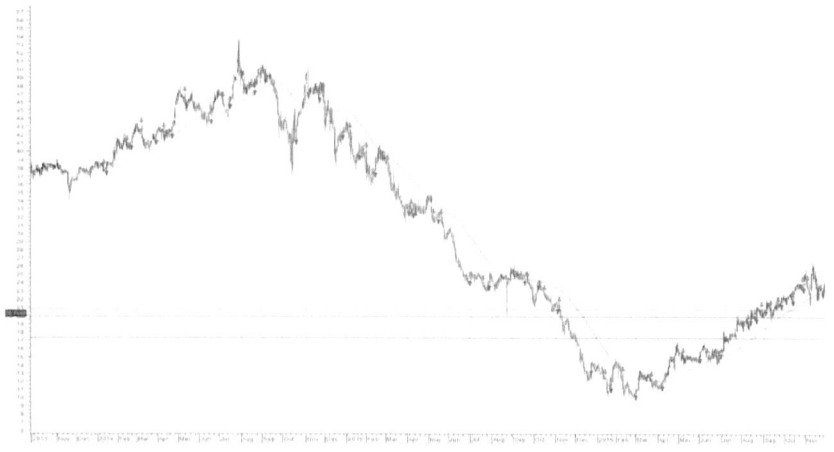

VOLUME

Volume shows how many trades are being made over specified period (usually day). If the volume is higher, you are probably going to be able to trade in/out faster as more people are buying/selling. Volume tells us number of shares that are being traded, it does not tell us if those traded are being bought or sold. We don't know exactly how many shares are being bought or sold but if you look at the stock price move substantially with high volume, you can guess if there are more sellers or buyers. If the stock price is moving up and the volume is higher you know there are more buyers putting money into that security. If the stock price is moving down and the volume is higher you can guess there are more sellers taking their money out of that security. Remember huge moves are usually fund managers who are deciding to take their money in or out. If you start to see stock price continue to rise but the volume is "drying out" getting less, you can assume that interest in that stock is getting less and thus maybe warning of a reversal. If the stock starts to decline with higher volume, you know that sellers are starting to sell. If you are having hard time figuring out if the volume is high or low, you can also have MAVG on volume and see if volume is higher or lower than the MAVG.

Some of the indicators relating to volume you may want to learn are: On-Balance Volume Indicator, Chaikin Money Flow and Klinger Volume Oscillator.

SUPPORT

Is a floor or base. It's historical price level at which stock no longer falls but either moves sideways or reverses up. Crossing of support level is a key alert for technical traders. Chart below shows "HALL" chart with support at $10.

RESISTANCE

Resistance is the ceiling which stock prices can't break above. A price at which the security has hard time breaking through. Once this price is reached stocks usually move sideways or start to reverse direction and move down. Chart below shows "HALL" chart with resistance at $11.75.

This is a 3-day chart of "HALL" from Jan 1, 2016 to Dec. 31st, 2017

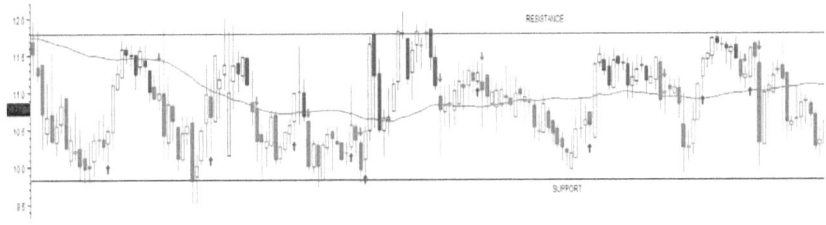

TRENDLINES

There is no stock that moves continuously straight up or straight down. In upward trend (bull trend) stocks usually rise, consolidate (move sideways) and then move back up in staircase. In downward trend (bear trend) stocks move down, consolidate and move down again. They may do this again and again to form a trend. In a rising stock, you can connect/draw a line at the lows of the stock price (as seen below) to form a rising trendline. Same can be done on dropping stock to form a declining trendline. If you can figure out this pattern, you can better understand your entry points and understand if this a bull or bear market/stock.

RSI: RELATIVE STRENGTH INDEX:

The relative strength index (RSI) is a technical indicator developed by J. Welles Wilder. RSI can be used as a momentum indicator, but it is graphed as an oscillator. Most importantly it is used to show you overbought (too many investors have bought this security and soon investors will start to take the profit and thus stock should decline) and oversold (too many investors have sold this security and soon investors will start to buy the stock, since it's a bargain and the price should rise) condition. Traditionally the RSI is considered overbought when above 70 and oversold when below 30, however you can modify these settings to fit your chart, some also use the setting 80/20.

The below chart is "T" AT&T from 2013-2018. The top part is RSI and the bottom part is the price of the stock. RSI has two horizontal lines at 30 (bottom) and 70 (top). The vertical lines are drawn anytime RSI is >70 or <30. This chart illustrates that when RSI <30, the stock price is oversold and thus should be bought and will rise and when RSI>70, it is overbought and thus should be sold as price will drop. Again, bear in mind no one indicator will be right all the time as in this case, however it does illustrated how RSI could possibly be used to show overbought/oversold condition.

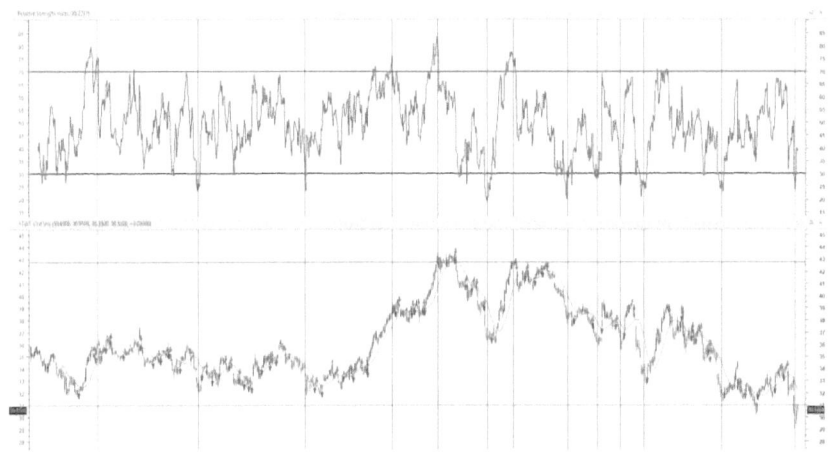

MACD

Moving Average Convergence Divergence is a momentum indicator that shows the relationship between two moving averages of prices. At first this may seem over complicated, but let's break it down.

The MACD is usually calculated by subtracting the 26-day

exponential moving average (EMA) from the 12-day EMA, this would be your MACD line.

A 9-day EMA of the MACD Line is plotted with the indicator, it's called the signal line. It is primarily used to see the trend.

The MACD-Histogram measures the difference between MACD and its 9-day EMA. The histogram is positive when MACD is above its signal line and negative when MACD is below its signal line.

Source: Tradermatt at the English language Wikipedia outlines MACD

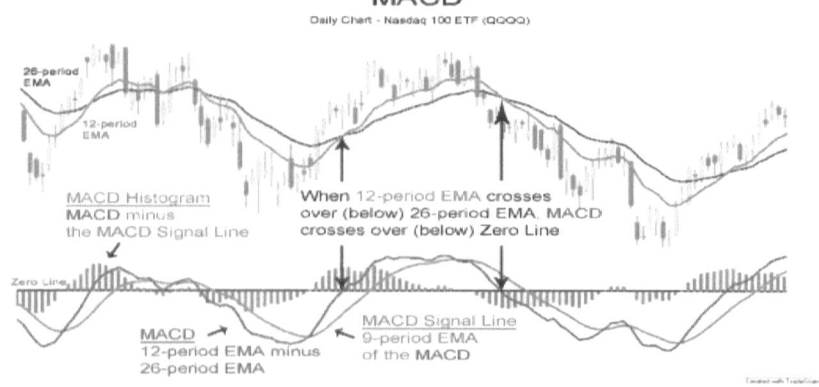

SUMMARY

There are 100's of indicators on the market today, you can literally spend years learning their equations and mathematical calculations. As you gain more expertise, you can add more of them to your arsenal, and weed out the ones that are over complicated without giving you any new information. For example, there are several momentum indicators, several oscillators, etc. If you are using 1 momentum you don't need to use other momentum indicators, this will tell you pretty much the same thing. I want you to use this section as a building block of what you learned in fundamental analysis. You can slowly see the whole system coming together.

Chapter 7: This is a VERY powerful chapter for all short-term traders. I can write book on this alone. However, I wanted to present this book as a comprehensive book that covers all aspect of investing/trading.

CHAPTER 7: POWERFUL TESTED STRATEGIES YOU CAN TRADE ON TODAY!

All advance investors apply various strategies to their portfolio. Like magician, most investors won't share their secret tricks of the trait, until of course it's not a secret anymore. I can't say I have a magic formula or a secret sauce. However, I've been trading for 30 years, and along with my mistakes, I also learned some strategies through just trial and error.

In my sincere attempt to take you from novice to advance investor in one book, I like to introduce some of the basic, yet powerful strategies that can make huge difference in your investments. We will keep most of these strategies straight forward and basics, but powerful (I also have more advance strategies that are overly complicated and may write its own book, sometime in the future).

Back Test Every Strategy Before Implementation

Back-test simply means go back in the past (1yr, 2yrs, 5yrs, 10yrs, how back in the past depends on how long in the future you would like to hold this security. Is it a quick in/out or are you planning on holding this for a while?) and to see how often you would have made/loss money applying this strategy. Some strategies work great on some stock but not on others, so back-test it.

If you went back 1 year, invested $1,000 and implemented a strategy (discussed below) and realized you would have been right 3 times and wrong 1 time and you would have made $200. Then you can go back 2yrs, 5yrs, 10yrs and see how you would have done. If you back tested and the results are positive, then you can attempt to introduce that strategy into that security. <u>Remember not all strategies work on all security & there are no guarantees; the minute you apply a strategy and it doesn't work, back-test again to make sure its still the best strategy available. Therefore, its pertinent that you back-test with enough data, to ensure that the odds are definitely in your favor!</u>

STRATEGY 1

<u>Moving Average Strategy</u>
One of the most used and most effective strategy is the moving average (MAVG).
This strategy is used to gauge the direction of the trend. Moving average, averages out series of market close and plots them. For example, a 10-day MAVG will take last 10 closes and averages them out and plots them. Therefore, if the market is moving up, the average of closes will also rise.

Once you plot the MAVG, if the trend of the stock is moving up the MAVG will also be moving up but will be below the stock price rising steadily under the stock price. If the stock price is trending down, you will see the MAVG above the stock price falling with the stock price.

Go ahead, plot a moving average and look! This is the best way to learn!

Magic happens when the stock price and MAVG cross each other, this signifies change of a trend. Thus, in this strategy one would buy and hold a stock as long as MAVG is below the stock price, and when the stock price crosses MAVG and MAVG is now above the stock, one would sell as this signifies a downward trend!

Contrary when the stock crosses the MAVG and starts to climb above the MAVG, this would signify a buy signal.

In this strategy, you would look for cross of MAVG with stock price and buy/sell on this signal over and over. You would rinse/repeat.

Below is a chart of CMI from 3/2015 to 12/2017 with a 100-day MAVG. I would sell as price goes below MAVG and buy as price comes above MAVG.

Most common MAVG plots are for 10-day, 20-day, 25-day, 50-day, 100-day and 200-day.

Which MAVG should you use?

You can try few of them and back-test to see if any fit the chart, sometimes it's trial and error.

Typically, you would use 10-day MAVG for short-term investing and 200-day MAVG for long-term investing i.e., retirement account. Also note that the nature of every stock is also different. Some stocks are more volatile (move up/down quickly) and if you use shorter MAVG it will give more buy/sell signal, you may not want to go in and out of position during market volatility. The best way to figure out which MAVG is right is to do back-testing. Look how many times you would have won/loss and how much you would have profited using a

10-day, 50-day MAVG.

STRATEGY 2

<u>Channeling Stocks</u>

No matter how much research you do, some stocks just titter-totter! In previous example, if you had purchased "HALL" on Jan 1, 2016 around $11.75 and held on to it until to Dec. 31st, 2017, its worth at $10.25. There would be no major win or loss. If I bought and held this stock, I would not have made any money.

You can see within this timeframe, the stock reached $11.50 at least 7 times and it reached $10.25 at least 7 times. What if I bought it around $10.25 and sold it at $11.50 seven times?

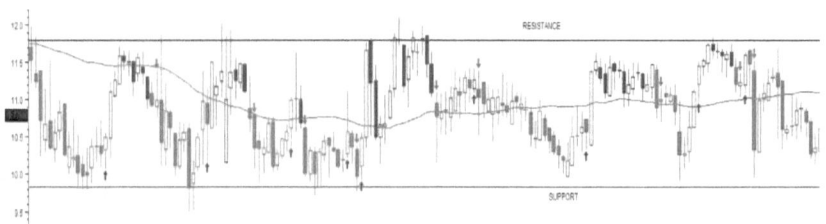

In this strategy you would find stocks such as these and continue to buy and sell them at price interval. I've done this for last 2yrs on this stock. You would find the resistance and support and buy and sell them repeatedly.

You would probably not want to be too greedy by waiting for the stock to come all the way down or all the way up, you want most touches at resistance and support. To prevent further loss, you may want to have another deep support in case the stock turns on you and gets out of the channeling pattern.

There are some stocks that are just not buy and hold stocks. Don't fight them, just look at the chart, if you noticed these patterns, don't think that because you bought them, and you did your research they are going to shoot for the moon. For example, if you look at AT&T "T", Early 2000 the stock was worth approx. $40, and end of 2017 the stock is worth about $40. Last 18 years there has been so much news, so many rumors, etc., don't fight the chart, even if this stock rises to $100, there are many good performers out there, don't fight 20 years of history. In defense of "T", this may not be completely accurate since "T" is known to provide great dividends, but nonetheless dividend can be taken away at any time the company decides to.

STRATEGY 3

RSI-Relative Strength Index
RSI is usually plotted for 14 days, with a two horizontal lines at 20 and 80. A buy signal would be generated when RSI crosses

the oversold line (20). Sell signal are generated when RSI crosses the overbought line (80).

In this indicator, you really do need to pick the right stock. Some stocks appear to stay above or below the line for quite a while. When stocks do this, they are either on a down or uptrend, in that case this is not the best indicator to use. Other stocks remain between 20-80, these stocks don't give clear overbought or oversold condition. Ideally you would want to see stocks with spikes above or below the lines and drop back down. This may be stated rather simplistic, and in my experience, you can't rely on this unless you have back tested (as with any of the other strategies, but especially this one). This strategy does not work well with many stocks. This may be a good secondary strategy, if you are on the fence about getting in/out, and you need some additional reassurance, consider RSI and see if it's below 20 or above 80 and then back-test to see if it has been reliable.

In this example I'm using BRKb, with 35/70 RSI. I am putting an order to sell anytime RSI reaches above 70 and will buy when RSI reaches below 35. My buy orders are more accurate than my sell order. Many times, after I sold a stock, it continues to rise. In this case I can possibly buy the stock when it reaches below 35 but use another indicator to sell. Red lines show the RSI is less than 35 and will be buying and blue line indicates I will be selling. You may get multiple buy signals and multiple sell signals, therefore don't sell all your holdings at once, but sell them in batches. If you have 300 shares, sell 100 each time.

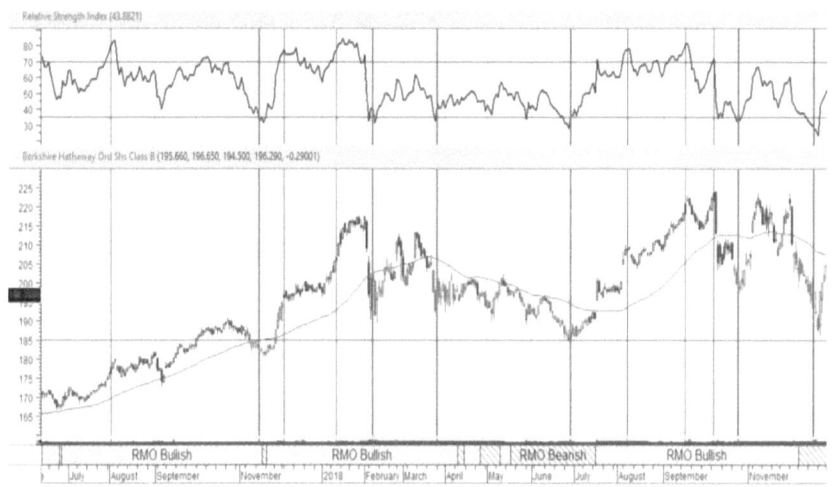

STRATEGY 4

<u>Trailing Stop Strategy-Prevent your losses and lock in your profits!</u>
This strategy works well with stocks that are momentum/trendy stocks. Stocks that tend to show you a diagonal line up are ideally the best ones. Once you have made some money in the stock, this strategy will secure your profit and ensure you won't lose but gaining all upside potential if the stock goes up. Here is how the strategy works.

This strategy involves placing a stop loss order. A stop loss is an order to sell stock, once it reaches a certain price. A stop-loss is designed to limit an investor's loss on a security position.

Once you are in the position (you own the stock). And the stock has risen, you will place stop loss below the fluctuation of the stock and/or below the previous support. The stock naturally fluctuates, it doesn't go straight up or straight down, it moves in zig zag (fluctuation). You want to put stop loss order below the fluctuation and below the previous support, this will give stock some chance to fluctuate without you being sold out! If the stock changes trend and begins to dive on you, your stop loss order gets activated and your stock is sold (making whatever profit you have made thus far on the stock or if you just bought it, you may have some loss based on risk you were willing to take). If the stock goes up, you are still in the position and now you will cancel the old order and move the stop loss order up, locking in your profit!

Let's say 1st you did your homework and found a momentum stock with diagonal chart, of course there are no guarantee the charts will continue its trend up, but we are going to assume it's going to continue what it has done in the past. You see chart for 'MA' appears to fit that model. So, you buy 'MA" for around $100 in September 2016. You will then place your stop loss below the last support, which is around $94 (where the horizontal line is placed). If the stock goes below $94, your trade will get executed and you will sell the stock for $6 loss! Therefore, that is your risk, you will never lose more than $6 per share in this example and you must be willing to take that risk. However, if the stock goes up (as we predict based on prior historical chart) you will be raising the stop loss, locking in the profit until stock goes below your stop loss order. As the stock is rising, I'm raising in my stop loss, as you can see with horizontal lines. On December 1st, 2016, my stop los order is executed at approx. $145. I did not get the high price of $155 just few days ago, however $100 to $145 in approximately 2 years is a good return.

There are broker's sites that allows you to input %/$ trailing stop value, which is constantly raised automatically certain % or $ below the market price. The stop-loss order is adjusted continually based on fluctuations in the market price, always maintaining the same percentage below the market price.

STRATEGY 5

<u>Buy on Dips!</u>

This is a risky strategy! In this strategy, you want to be careful to own ETF or solid stocks, you plan to own. We are going to look at the same "MA" stock as we did in strategy 4. In this strategy, we are going to add to our position every time the stock dips below MAVG. We will be incorporating 40-day MAVG into this chart. Every time stock dips below 40day-MAVG will we be buying or adding to our position. In another words we will be buying on dips when the stock comes down and will accumulate much more at this price. You can see the potential return, following this strategy!

Reason this is a risky strategy, is because if you are buying on dips, what happens when a dip turns into a long-term bear market? This is the reason you want to own ETF or great companies that around for a long time, because you want to be certain that these companies are going to bounce back! Secondly, you want to purchase these great companies at a lower price is because they are a bargain! If you did valuation calculation from prior chapter, you would know if they are a bargain or not!

Other cons to this strategy is if the market is going to dip for a while, you must have enough capital to continue to purchase on down market and be able to hold a long time!

Despite above reasons, you still may not want your capital tied up for extensive amount of time in down market. In that case you need to have an exit strategy, which will alert you to buy on dips but get out during bear market! We are going to do this by introducing a 2nd MAVG to the same chart. This MAVG is going to be 100-day MAVG. In this example we will be buying on dip below 40-day MAVG but will be selling it all at 100-day MAVG. You need to make sure that touches at 40-day MAVG are a lot more than at 100-day MAVG, as you don't want to sell all frequently. Of course, you can modify/adjust MAVG to fit the right stock.

There is also a third indicator, however in my opinion not that reliable, "Death Cross". It is basically when 50-day MAVG crosses below the 200-day MAVG. You can back test it to see if this is a profitable indicator for a particular security.

STRATEGY 6

<u>Reversal Catch</u>

Nobody has a crystal ball; you will even find brainiest guys/gals arguing on CNBC in a language you don't even understand. Surely, they must know more than you know. They are throwing out terms that are in a foreign language. Follow them, see their picks and you will realize they are wrong half of the times. Hell, you can be right 50% of the time too. When a lot of money is on the line and your emotions are high, you will react to stock market fluctuation more than sticking to your own strategy!

You will sell when you are supposed to buy and buy when you are supposed to sell. I advise you to stick to your strategy, with clear buy/sell signals before you enter the position. Let's say you are still wrong, or the volatility of the market, gets you out of the market/into the market and then takes off in the opposite direction! This has happened to me several times. I would own a security, let's say XYZ-$55 and it starts to go down on me, I had clear direction to sell, so I put a stop loss at $50, the price comes down to $49.96, I'm sold out of the position. I stop following it for a while and after 6 mos. I look at the price and it's $150! When this happened few times, I started to develop a strategy called "Reversal Catch". In this strategy, once I get stopped out, let's say at $49.96, I continue to follow the stock <u>more vigilantly than before</u>!!! To make sure execution of my trade was not just due to stock volatility but a long-term downtrend, and all my other reason to sell this stock were valid.

If the price is turning on me and headed in opposite direction I will get back into this position! Yes, I will lose some money since most likely I will now get sold out at $49.96 and will probably buy based on certain other parameters at higher price, possibly like $55. I also won't just randomly get back into the position. One it has to be that I just got stopped out on the volatility of the market and all other conditions are the same. Secondly, I must have clear reason to enter the position again. At times I will have reevaluate the condition before rebuying the stock, sometimes I will anticipate reversal catch buy price before even selling the stock. I may need to have reversal entry price points to be defined, for example crossing of MAVG, or breaking previous resistance or another indicator that I was following before I got sold out. It's hard for me to have the exact entry points here, but just know it's ok to lose some money and get back in/out of position than to have the wrong trade executed. Now, you most likely will lose money doing this trade, since you will probably have purchased/sold at the wrong time and you are buying/selling this at higher/lower price than you wanted to. This is ok, especially if this is a long-term position. Even in semi short-term position (1-6 months), this could be ok. Don't be stubborn, if the market turns on you, or you just got sold out at the bottom, don't be afraid to re-evaluate and hop back on even for some short-term loss! Don't sit on the sideline, hoping the market continues in one direction because you are in/out of the position, market doesn't know when you bought/sold the stock, and frankly the market doesn't care!

STRATEGY 7

Stop Buy Order

In earlier strategy, we discussed the stop loss order, if you are in a position and the market starts to go down, you enter a stop loss order, a price at which you will get out of the position. But what is a stop buy order?

In a stop buy order you are purchasing security when it hits a strike price that is higher than the current price. Once the price hits specific price outlined on the trade, the stop buy becomes a market order. The buy-on-stop price always is set above the existing market price.

For example, stock XYZ is at $95, I place a stop buy order at $100, when the stock goes from $95 to $100, I will purchase the stock at $100! Uhm mm...why should I wait for the stock to go up to $100, when I can buy the stock at $95 (for cheaper) today?

This all depends on your overall plan. We know that many stocks move in trends/consolidate/trends.

For example, this stock is at $45, rises and remains between $60-$65, then rises and remains between $75-$80 and then drops and stays between $65-$70 then rises to $95-$100. At this time, you don't know if the stock is due for a drop or rise, however based on its pattern you assume that if it breaks $100, its due for a climb up. Therefore, you only want to purchase this stock if it breaks the $100 marker!

Another reason could be, that at $100 it is going break a MAVG, and you noticed that once it breaks a MAVG it continues to climb up but if it doesn't then it drops!

Stop buy traders believe this prevents them from buying early in uncertainty, and they are ok with less profit, because they believe it gives them higher assurance.

STRATEGY 8

Time Frame

Today many television programs, magazines, newspapers and online articles sensationalize the news. They are in the market of selling their product, not necessarily informing you of the truth. This is obvious in today's political culture; exaggerated one sided story broadcasted to create emotional anguish. This is also true of the stock market news, to lesser extent. Every small move in the market, is presented to you as doomsday! This creates panic that makes you want to tune in and worst has you go in/out of market, when you shouldn't be. The following strategy will help you rules out lots of noise and volatility that may happen every day and instead focus on larger, more significant movements of the security or the market. Of course, if you are day trader or very short-term trader, you probably won't want to use this method.

Some stocks have a trend but it's hard to see and when you apply an indicator is so hard make sense of it on the chart. The security seems to go all over the chart. It is too erratic to fit any MAVG or a good indicator. GOOG is one such example.

This is a daily chart of GOOG from June 2015-Dec. 2018 with 50-day MAVG. You can see the crossing of the MAVG frequent. If you are using MAVG as your indicator in this example, you will be going in and out unnecessarily and frequently.

Most all charts are defaulted as a daily chart. You will find that you can modify charts setting to weekly, monthly or even custom days. In some cases, when you change these settings, it may seem like you are looking at brand new security. You may get a lot clearer view of the behavior of the stock. It may allow all indicator to fall in place.

This is GOOG on weekly chart with the same 50-day MAVG.

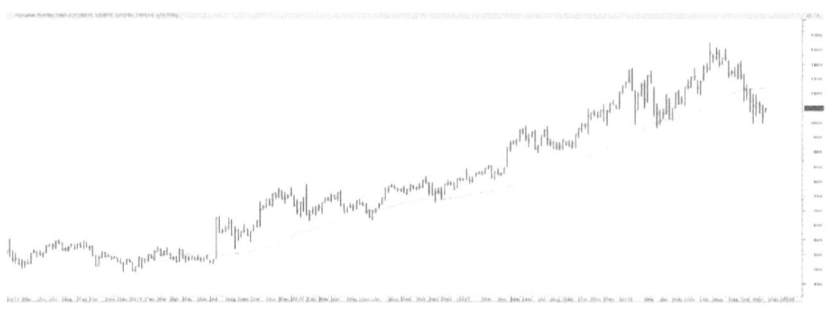

You can see this will yield a lot better predictor of a trend; it will cut out daily noise. This will prevent you from going in and out of the security unnecessary. You will also be better able to predict larger trend and not panic on every move the stock is making.

All securities are different, but if the charts aren't making good trendy sense, try adjusting the frequency to 3-day, weekly, bi-weekly and on occasion monthly (long term 401k funds).

Some of these strategies are contradictory to other strategies. For example, RSI > 80 will tell you to sell but what if at the same time price has just crossed above MAVG then which in one of the strategies should you follow? That's why it's pertinent that you back-test your performance for each strategy you are implementing, to see historically how many times has the RSI>80 and MAVG crossed the price and which strategy prevailed most of the time. If this happened 50-50% of the time, none of those strategies are reliable. This is critical because some stocks exhibit certain behavior. Not all these strategies may work for you, and not all strategies work on all securities. You really do have to spend some time applying the right strategies, right settings to right security. This will take some time. You may have to tweak some of the strategies. As you get more confidant, you will start to add your own nuance to these strategies or create your own that works for you. But what if you tried several strategies and none of them fit that security? MOVE ON! There are approx. 4,000 stocks you can invest in.

As you get better and understand different indicators and what they mean, you can add multiple strategies to form one strategy. For example, you may only get into the position at crossing of 2 MAVG and RSI is just coming over 30 on a weekly chart but you may sell when RSI > 80. I can write almanac on all different scenarios; I hope this has opened your eyes on various possibilities.

SUMMARY - UNDERSTANDING THE WHOLE SYSTEM

I've promised you, earlier in this book that it's my objective to take you from a beginner to investing like a professional. I tried to provide you much as content with truth as I know.

This is overall plan in a nutshell. Of course, we can dive deep into each one of these concepts. However, this book should leave you with overall summary of investing. It has taken me a long time to learn some of these concepts, and I hope you find them useful. It was my aim to cut out lot of noise and irrelevant information that you are constantly bombarded with on the internet about "click here to make millions" that play to your emotions. I wanted to write a book that opens up newbie's eyes to world of investing. I wanted to help them understand the foundation, various styles of investing/trading, learn some key fundamental and technical concept, implement several strategies at the same time reveal some of the misconception. This should equip you with basics of investing.

If this is your first-time trading, start with paper money, then move to small trades than large ones. You can start with these principals and ultimately create your own principals of trading and don't get diverted with so much noise out there.

You should have understanding on where to find stocks, how to screen them, research them, do fundamental analysis on them, value them, do technical analysis on them and apply strategies.

Remember stocks usually go down faster than they climb up. You may see a sudden drop more frequent than sudden rise. It is because of this, panic sets in and may cause a rational person to become irrational. But NOT you! You are a disciplined investor. You have a plan! You will have prepared for each scenario, know your exit points, and entry points (even with small losses). You are NOT worried, you are going to stick to your plan-write it down, not kind of have it in your head! This doesn't mean you can't change/shift to moving market, but you must know why you are making these changes, and it's not on emotions alone but on sound reasoning. You will learn to modify and document that plan as needed, but not trade haphazardly! Remember you are not losing/winning until you get out of the position.

At the end, you know you've done enough research and have created your plan before you entered the position, therefore you are not going to buy and hope but execute your plan. It's like a pro athlete, who has practiced all his/her life, and when the game is on the line, he/she is just going to execute what he/she has been taught and done thousands of times.

I hope that this book has planted an "Aha" seed! I have introduced the whole package to you. These are powerful concepts and real-life knowledge, but don't stop here! Build on the concept here, there is always more to learn and I don't claim to know it all! It is my hope you become independent thinker who builds on this knowledge.

Having said all of this, you will have losses! Your emotions will play a role, especially when you have a lot of money riding on a trade! You don't learn swimming by reading a book, and you won't learn trading by reading a book. You will have to trade to become a better trader. However, you have just cut out years from someone who is not equipped with this knowledge!

I've attempted to instill some principals and commonly used methods and strategies. Even if you don't use a strategy or a concept in this book, you will have good support to build on moving forward. Down the line, you can create your own, think on your own, and bring something to table. I hope this book has been a good resource for you. I've done my best to break things down. If this book has added value to you, I look forward to your review.

Good Investing!

LEARN MORE AT
WWW.INVESTINGPRODIGY.COM

www.ingramcontent.com/pod-product-compliance
Lightning Source LLC
Chambersburg PA
CBHW021451210526
45463CB00002B/731